RIP SOME LIPS

FISH TAILS AND OTHER STORIES FROM ALASKA

By

J. KEVIN CURRY

1663 LIBERTY DRIVE, SUITE 200
BLOOMINGTON, INDIANA 47403
(800) 839-8640
WWW.AUTHORHOUSE.COM

© 2005 J. KEVIN CURRY. All Rights Reserved.

No part of this book may be reproduced, stored in a retrieval system, or transmitted by any means without the written permission of the author.

First published by AuthorHouse 03/25/05

ISBN: 1-4208-2747-2 (sc)

Library of Congress Control Number: 2005901284

Printed in the United States of America
Bloomington, Indiana

This book is printed on acid-free paper.

Dedication

Dedicated to:

Cindy, Monopoly, Barley, Remington, and Whiskey Burchfield.

Special thanks to:

Daren Powers, Daniel Berg, Reid Mullins, Harlan Furbush, Jerry and Carol Dana, and any family member that ever went fishing and hunting with me!

Front cover painting "Rip Some Lips" by Cindy Burchfield Used by permission.

Shakedown Cruise...

It was supposed to be your run of the mill "Shakedown" cruise, the first fishing trip of the new year, but then again nothing is ever run of the mill in Alaska!

The motors were running great, the day was overcast, and the water was flat! The lines were baited and thrown overboard just because there was nothing else better to do!

The mighty Alaskan King Salmon was minding her own business when all Hell broke loose! If you are curious how I know it was a she, well, the best way to tell is to rip it open from bunghole to snout and look for eggs! No eggs, it's a dude! Eggs, well I think you know the rest! I'm sure she was just looking for a "free lunch", but we all know there is no such thing as a "free lunch"!

The reel started screamin'! And I shouted "Fish On", and the game was a foot! Cindy was so excited that she had trouble bringing up the other rod and downrigger so I told her to forget the rod and just deal with the downrigger! With the downrigger up she went for the net, only to find that it would not lock into the extended position! She would have to improvise! I brought the fish to the boat and the she salmon ran like mad! She darted across the back of the boat and became hooked on the other line that was still in the water and she ran for the bottom! Now both reels are screaming! We have both now caught the same fish! I brought her back to the boat and this time she was close enough for Cindy to get the net on so she was ours!

I clubbed her and gutted her, and we ate her! She was great! Monopoly, our Scotty dog, was able to do her favorite thing in the world once again, lick the slime off of a King Salmon!

The first King of the year is always the best! Our black lab, Remington, watched this whole event with much fascination; I can't help but wonder what he was thinking as

I was clubbing that mighty fish! I'm sure it was something like this, "Boy, I don't really know what you just did but you really pissed off Pa!"

Have a great day and welcome to spring in Alaska!

Cindy, Monopoly, and a King!

It takes a village....

It was a beautiful summer evening when our friends Jerry and Carol Dana called and said let's go drag a herring around and have dinner on the boat. Sounds like a great plan! The water was flat and the evening sky was filled with blue and pink reflections of the Chilkat range.

The lines were in the water and the steak was on the grill. Margaritas, gin and tonic, and of course beer were in good supply.

We were just starting to enjoy our steak sandwiches when the silence was broken by the greatest sound of all, a screaming fishing reel! Cindy shouted, "Fish on" and all five of us lunged for the rod! I set the hook and the fish continued to run.

I was able to coax the mighty beast around and started to bring it up to the boat. Once the King saw the boat he ran like Hell and the reel gave way!

"Oh shit!" The reel had backlashed and looked more like the back of Coolio's head than a fishing reel!

Jerry, the captain of the boat, said, "We are not losing this one!" And I handed the rod over to Carol and it was my turn to be the reel! That's right! I started working the fish up to the boat with my bare hands. Carol would pull back on the rod and I would hold the line tight and then she would dip the rod down and I would "reel" in the line with my hands.

Luckily the fish only ran a couple more times. Each time I would let the line go, running over my palms, just waiting for a sign that the run was over and we would start the process over again.

When the fish finally got close enough to the boat Jerry started assisting me by switching the kicker in and out of reverse and Cindy grabbed the net. We, and I do mean WE, landed the fish only to find out that it was just legal! Twenty-eight inches exactly! And it was a "White" King salmon! Oh yeah! That was one tasty fish!

Speaking of food. While all of this transpired our friend's dog, Zhanna ate all of our steak sandwiches! No wonder she was not in the way!

Salmon cop a feel...

After a hard day at the office there is nothing better than hitting the old fishing hole to relax. Besides with a little luck you might just catch something and get to take out your frustrations killing the crap out of it!!

In Juneau the sun does not shine all that often so when it does you must get out and enjoy it. The day I had at the office simply sucked! So the second I got off work I drove straight to Montana Creek for a little therapy.

Standing beside my truck, parked just on the side of the road, I ripped off my cubicle jockey suit and jumped into my waders. Of course the waders, fly rod, vest, net, and insect repellent were in the truck. One never goes anywhere without those items. Especially the bug spray!

Anyway, I hiked downstream to my favorite holding pool and waded in up to my chest. God I love glacier runoff! Nothing like 38 degree water to get the old blood pumping!

I started to cast. Cast and retrieve. Cast and retrieve... Nothing! I couldn't even get anything to rise. It couldn't possibly be that I don't know how to fish. I do. Change flies, that's the answer! Cast and retrieve. Cast and retrieve...Oh well I have completely forgotten about the sucky day I was having a few hours ago!

Fly fishing in Montana Creek

An eagle swooped right up the creek, over my head and landed in a tree overlooking the water about 200 yards away. I continue to cast and retrieve. The eagle mocks me by leaping from its perch and snatching up a trout no more that 100 yards from me! Ah ha! There are fish in this damn creek!

I cast again and I feel something rub against my leg! I look down to see if a branch has drifted downstream and caught on my waders only to find that an entire school of Silver salmon is swimming all around me! They are rubbing against both legs! I start to retrieve my fly in at a frantic pace to try to catch one of these glorious beasts and two of them almost knock me down by swimming right between my legs!

I fished for another hour with nary a bite. That's all I really remember about that terrible day. There is nothing like getting felt up by a Ho. A Coho that is!!!

Just a shimmy up the mountain...

Bush pilots in Alaska are insane! They firmly believe they are ten feet tall and bulletproof! They also are optimistic to a fault. They believe they can land anywhere and takeoff from just about anywhere and amazingly enough about 99% of the time they are right.

We have a good friend, Mike Jackson that is a bush pilot. We love to go hunting with him every chance we get. It's always a good time and a great adventure!

Not too long ago we were over in Hoonah, AK deer hunting by day and staying in Mike's mother's B&B by night. His mother, Jan Jackson is quite the character too!

Anyway, the only fur bearing creatures we had been able to find were far more interested in eating me than the other way around. There are so many bears over on Chicagof Island you can just about throw a rock and hit one.

The night before the last day of hunting, we were back at the B&B enjoying a hot shower and some of Jan's wonderful grub when Mike suggested that we take off with him in the morning. That meant flying and landing where no one had ever landed before. Oh yeah!

This also meant we were about to be treated to more of Mike's undying optimism! You see we learned a long time ago that Mike suffers from a disease we call "Mike Vision". What is "Mike Vision" you ask? Well, he is known for spotting a deer on top of a mountain and saying, "I'll put the plane down over there and we will just shimmy up that HILL and boom! Pop Bambi! It's just a quick five or ten minute hike!" Anytime he says that you are guaranteed a three hour climb that will involve ropes, oxygen, and a daring Coast Guard Rescue!

The next morning we take off! We fly around for about thirty minutes and we get to the mountain that Mike has picked out for our adventure. Sure enough we spot deer on the backside of the peak and he starts looking for a suitable strip for crash landing!

"There it is" he says and then those wonderful words we have all been waiting for, "I'll put the plane down over there and we will just shimmy up that HILL and boom! Pop Bambi! It's just a quick five or ten minute hike!" Here we go! Alert the Coast Guard!

The "strip" he has chosen is maybe 500 feet long and is sloped, I'm being very kind there, up the mountain. As we are coming in for a trial run, no landing this time, we spot another nice deer just below the end of the "strip". Did I mention the end of the "strip" is a cliff!

Mike pulls up at the last possible second and we circle around for the real thing this time. He shouts out that we are on "Final" and put the plane down! We buck and pitch and bounce and finally stop just before we collide with a boulder the size of a Dodge truck at the end of the "strip" and Mike says to get after it.

The strip.

Cindy and I get out of the plane and sure enough it is at least 1500 feet straight up to the top of the peak. Who cares! We are so pumped on adrenalin right now I think we could climb Denali!

Cindy after the shimmy!

We actually do "just shimmy up the Hill" and when we get to the top and stop to catch our breath we realize, "Holy Crap! We have to climb back down this sucker! What the Hell were we thinking!"

RIP SOME LIPS

The white dot in the center is our plane.

We sneak on down to the spot where the deer WERE! We work our way around the peak but no luck. We hear a rifle shot and figure at least Mike got one so there will be fresh backstrap on the menu tonight so we start making our way back to the crash, eh I mean landing site.

Mike missed so there will be no venison for any of us tonight.

We climb back into the plane and get ready for takeoff. I start assessing the amount of runway we have to work with and quickly figure out that there most definitely is not enough! Mike gives the plane full throttle and is grinning from ear to ear as we go ripping down the way too short "strip"! At the end of the "strip" the plane does not takeoff like you would expect, no it just dives right off the cliff that is the end of the "strip"! We drop a good ways before we have enough airspeed to actually climb out of the valley we have just entered!

I swallow two times! It took both swallows to get my asshole back on the inside of my body!

We circle back around and there they are those bastard deer! Oh well! Another day!

After another night at the B&B and some of Jan's moose stroganoff it's back to Juneau!

Boat launching anyone...

Ah, fishing season is finally in full swing! I love fishing season! There is nothing better than catching, gutting, filleting, cooking, and eating fresh King Salmon right off the grill! Served of course with an ice cold homebrew or Alaskan Summer Ale!

But there is one thing that comes close and that is watching all the idiots try to load/unload their boats down at the boat launch! Sometimes I go out to Auke Bay just for a little Alaskan Wildlife Viewing. Gnashing of teeth, cursing, and a busted tail light makes for a great evening.

For every one person that knows how to back a trailer there must be five that obviously would have difficulty walking or remembering to breathe!

I, personally, have never experienced this problem. I always back my trailer with skill and grace. I always, uh-oh, I think I just forgot something, gasp, gasp, gasp, oh sweet oxygen! That's much better! So for a good time head on down to your local boat launch, kick back, and enjoy! And don't forget to breathe!

How to catch crabs...

If you spend any time at all fishing in Alaska you will probably end up pulling a crab pot or two. This is a good thing! Don't be afraid of the pots. The crab are your friends. Why not, they taste great! There is truly nothing like eating fresh King crab right out of the cooker. The only thing that comes close is fresh Dungies out of the cooker.

First you have to spend about a bazillion dollars on a good boat. Then about a bazillion dollars on pots, line, buoys, and a good pot puller. Yes you can pull them by hand if YOU want to but after you have done that once you too will come over to the dark side! I've done it and it was dumb! Enough said!

A pot full of fun!

Next you need to buy a good supply of beer or scotch so you will be able to get your buddy drunk enough to tell you where to set your pots. Beware! This may take a lot more beer or scotch than you think and you better not use the cheap stuff either! Cheap stuff will only yield information on really crappy fishing holes!

Now get your buddy drunk without getting yourself too drunk to remember where he told you to fish. This can be very tricky as most Alaskans can really hold their booze. It's something about the long cold winters that builds this tolerance!

You've got the information so now it is time to go fishing! Blast out to the crab fishing grounds, which will probably be full of other pots! Bait those puppies up and drop them overboard.

If you buy me a case of good Alaskan Summer Ale I will tell you how deep to fish! All I will say is Dungies are shallow and Kings are deep!

When fishing for Kings you may also pick up a few Tanner crabs. These taste good too. Down south they are known as Snow crab but up here we call them Welfare crab! Why eat inferior crab when you can have all the King crab you want?

King crab!

Anyway drop the pots and let them soak for a while, once again I will gladly tell you how long for another case of Alaskan Summer Ale!

Pull them back up and there should be crab. If not then your buddy lied to you and you need to let him know by bringing over even more beer or scotch!

Take the crab home and it is time to cook them up. Bring a huge pot of water to a boil and now for some fun. It's time for the ceremonial naming of the crab! That's right we name each crab before we put them in the pot. We name them after our boss, a coworker, a government official, or anyone that has pissed you off that week!

I would tell you how long to cook them but that would require yet another case of beer!

Now it's time for the very best part...the eating! Don't be embarrassed but all of us Alaskans will laugh at you for the rest of the night! Why? Well, you will be doing the "Crab Dance"! It starts off with a smile that just looks stupid! Then your head and shoulders start to bounce like you are two years old! Then you will start to hum, "MMM MMM MMM"! Oh yeah! You are now "Crab Dancing" and everyone knows it!

Crab dancing.

Have another beer, wipe your hands on your pants, and grab another crab!!!

Maximum blood flow...

A couple of years ago my wife got a call from her sister that changed our lives. Her sister called and asked Cindy if she knew what our nephew Marty, her son, was getting for a graduation present? Of course Cindy said "no". Two round trip tickets for him and his best friend Buck to spend two weeks fishing with you!

With some degree of trepidation we did agree. You see we had not spent very much time with Marty over the years and had never even met Buck! All we really knew about them was that they were longhaired, tattooed, Slayer fans that wanted to go fishing/hunting! Besides, if things got really bad there could always be some sort of hunting accident! Alaska is a great place to make someone disappear!

A sign of things to come?

Anyway, they were perfect gentlemen and we had a blast!

We went Silver fishing and anyone that has ever gone Silver fishing will tell you sometimes instead of Silvers you catch a lot of Pink salmon. If you are up from down south and you don't know any better it's just a big fish to you! So it does not matter.

Those of us that do know better try to shake the Pinks off the line well outside of the boat as they can be quite messy! Pinks are bleeders! If they get cut in anyway they tend to spray blood like Old Faithful.

After the boys learned this fact they insisted that all of the Pinks come in the boat. I agreed only if they took them home and ate them, we don't waste fish, and if they cleaned the boat when we were done. They agreed and the carnage began!

Blood in the bilge!

Every fish that came into the boat was quickly dispatched in a manner that would insure maximum blood flow! Freddie Krueger had nothing on us! There was blood everywhere. On the motors, on the windshield, in my hair, our black lab Remington had an auburn hue! I kept looking over my shoulder for Wes Craven and his film crew. We were still finding evidence of that fishing trip two years later. And yes they did take all of the fish home.

The best part was Marty's insistence on being clean during this whole event. He did not like getting blood or fish slime on him in any way. Every time a fish came on board Marty would wash his hands. A big tough guy with the little fish but a wimp when it came to getting dirty! Go figure.

Check out those clean hands

On this same trip the boys really wanted to go camping. Since it was buck season, yes I realize one of the boys was named Buck but he was not in danger, his taxidermed carcass standing in the corner would just frighten the dogs, I agreed.

Here is a hint on how to get two teenage boys to listen to everything you say for at least 24 hours. LIE. It really works! Play on their fears and you will be in charge.

I chose to go camping on Lincoln Island for two reasons. Number one there is good deer hunting on that island and number two there are no bears on that island. None at all! Did I happen to tell them there were no bears on that island? No!

That afternoon we loaded up the boat and blasted over to Lincoln for the evening. Cindy dumped us on the beach and I told the guys to setup camp and I would be back in a couple of hours. I took off to see if I could find a buck.

I was gone almost three hours and when I returned the boys were still standing on the beach in the same location that I had left them at three hours earlier! All the gear was still piled up on the beach and no camp was made.

I asked what was going on and they said that they had heard something! "Must have been a bear!"

I talked them into setting up camp and we had a great evening of telling stories by the fire.

When bedtime rolled around I placed my rifle next to my bedroll and they watched me very carefully. I looked over at them and said, "Bear spray"!

The next morning I snuck out of the camp before dawn for a morning hunt. When I returned there those wimps were, sitting by the fire, eyes as wide as saucers! I guess they "heard something else"!

We broke camp and Cindy arrived to pick us up for another day of maximum blood flow on the water. But before the blood flowed we blasted over to Admiralty Island, just to mess with their feeble little minds a little more!

There are a lot of bears on Admiralty, I mean a lot! Just up the beach we found bear tracks that were about a foot across! I told the guys we should walk up the creek a ways and see what we find! They agreed but they would not take the lead! I tried to get them to take the lead but Marty said, "You've got the gun, you lead!" They may be wimps but I have to give them credit for not being dumb!

We went out and slayed some more fish and that night we went over to a friends house for a cookout. Our friends started asking the boys about all the bears over on Lincoln Island and they quickly figured out that they had been setup!

That's the night I became Uncle Asshole!

Just remember, it's okay to lie to teenage boys! They need it! And when they ask why you did it just tell them Uncle Asshole told you to do it!

Buck and his Silver!

J. KEVIN CURRY

Derby days...

Last year our nephew Zac came up to fish the Golden North Salmon Derby with us. For those of you that are not aware the Golden North Salmon Derby is the premier event in every fishing season. As young people like to say, "It's the shit!" I'm still not sold on that saying, in my mind "shit" is shit, but then again I don't want to be considered old either! But I digress.

Zac is a good looking kid, 18 years old, about 10 feet tall and bulletproof! And did I mention opinionated? Yes... Zac knows all!

But most of all he loves to fish! He is a lot of help on the boat too. He is not afraid to get dirty and he learns amazingly quickly for someone that already knows it all! Within just a few hours he was running lines and cutting bait like a pro!

On the first day of the Derby we ran out to Point Retreat to try our luck. The lines went in the water, one flat line, one medium line, and one deep line looking for that elusive King Salmon!

We trolled for about an hour and a half and didn't even get a bump then all Hell broke loose!

The Silvers started hitting and just would not stop! Every time a fish would come in the boat another rod would take off! We were having double and tripleheaders constantly!

No sooner than you could bait the hook and run it out it would take off. We had fish pulling lines out of the downriggers as they were going down! We didn't even have time to pee! And who cares! With action like that who needs to pee!

Next thing we knew we had 14 Silvers on board and the bite started to wane. I told the crew that we had enough Silvers. It's time to focus on Kings. So the lines went down deep. And we got to eat lunch and take a pee!

Silvers…That's what I'm talkin' about!

During this lull we were fortunate enough to be amazed and educated by the wonderful wisdom of Zac. He informed us that there are basically four types of people on the planet. There are the "Homo's", the "Tree Huggers", the "Tree Huggin' Homo's", and the "Cool". Lucky for me, I'm "Cool"!

He also let us know that it is okay for a woman to be a lesbian as long as she is hot! If she is not hot, well that's just nasty!

Now back to the fishing! In between all of these wonderful tidbits of knowledge we managed to pick up four more Silvers. We had then caught our limit for the day. So I suggested that we try one more spot and get serious about catching a King.

We pulled in the lines and headed for North Pass. Once there we forgot about the flat line and just fished deep. We trolled for about thirty minutes when my old trusty rig, a cut plug on a blue flasher, took off! The reel screamed like only a King can make it scream!

I told Cindy to grab the rod. She said "No, you catch it!" And I said, "Cindy catch that goddamned fish!" Why did I say it that way you ask? Well, in the boat we have a rule and that rule is; it's not serious unless it is prefaced by the word "goddamn". If you hear that word it means now! And yes it does work both ways. If she says it I jump!

She grabbed the rod and started the fight! The fight was awesome! That King ran three times.

After the third run the fish came to the boat and was ready to be netted. I grabbed the net and netted the fish. When I started to lift the fish into the back of the boat the net broke! Zac and I lunged over the motor and grabbed the sides of the net and brought that King on board! High fives all around!

Oh no!!!

It was huge! We knew we were going to be in the money with this one! So we made a beeline for Amalga Harbor.

The fish weighed in at 26.7 pounds! Cindy finished the Derby in 14th place and her prize was $750 worth of Snap

On tools. Yes we have all three wrenches proudly hanging on our wall!

We caught quite a few more fish that weekend but nothing like that first day. A great day of fishing even makes listening to a load of crap from an 18 year old okay!

Fishing with a friend...

Sometimes the morning just comes way too early. You really have no desire to get out of bed. The only thing on your mind at that very time is...sleep!

This happens to me from time to time. Usually after we have already put a few King Salmon in the freezer. I love to fish but sometimes you just need the rest. But apparently this is not acceptable!

I can't tell you how many times I have wanted to stay in bed only to hear my wife say, "Get up! We are going fishing!"

I have learned that arguing this issue will not work! When she wants to go fishing we are going fishing! Death would not even stop her from fishing. I honestly think if she came in the bedroom and found me dead she would load me in the boat and take me fishing! The fresh air would be good for me! And if I didn't happen to awaken from the dirt nap she would cut a plug out of my leg, make it swim just right, and catch a great big King Salmon!

I saw quickly that it was going to be one of those mornings so I gave up and we went fishing. Besides, I really didn't want to have a plug cut out of me!

We blasted out to Point Retreat and dragged a couple of herring back and forth between Point Retreat and Cordwood Creek. Nothing!

We fished for a good couple of hours without any hits at all. We killed the time by watching eagles soar and by watching the shore for bears or deer. No luck there either.

We decided to change holes so we started working our way back into North Pass. As we pulled into the pass we saw a large group of sea lions playing in the surf.

I told Cindy that those sea lions were there for a reason and right on cue a giant sea lion came out of the water up to his chest, right next to the boat, with a huge King Salmon in his mouth! He shook that fish just like a dog would shake your sock and slapped it against the water trying to kill it! It went down and came right back up and proceeded to devour that fish! It was awesome!

I turned to Cindy and said, "The fish are here! Let's fish!"

We dropped our lines in the water and started to troll. I pulled out my trusty baseball bat and made sure it was positioned in the back of the boat just in case I needed to swat a sea lion.

Less than five minutes later one of the rods took off! Oh yeah! Here we go!

I grabbed the rod and Cindy brought up all the gear. I could tell this was a very nice fish by the way it ran. Straight to the bottom!

I started to work the fish up and got about half way when it ran again. I was starting to get a little concerned about the sea lions. They will take a fish from you and not even say thanks!

On the third run I noticed that there were a few sea lions starting to take notice. I told Cindy to get the net ready; we may only have one chance to get it in the boat! She was ready and the mighty King was ours!

Just after the fish was in the boat I looked up to check on our hungry friends. They dove down about thirty feet from the back of the boat and resurfaced right off the side as if to say, "Next time buddy! Next time!"

Feed us!

There is nothing like catching a 33 pound King while being pursued by a predator!

The bat is for the Seal Lions.

Beach picnics...

Your first winter in Alaska makes all the difference. I believe that is why most Alaskans are a little standoffish with newbies that first winter. They want to see if you are really going to stay around or if this is just some passing fancy.

I have a theory that if a person does not like it here they will leave very quickly. No one decides to just stick it out. It's just not worth it. Therefore the majority of the people here are here because they like it here. They like the cold, dark, rain, snow, bamboo under the fingernails lifestyle that Alaska provides! In short, we are a bunch of really sick puppies up here!

Amazingly your second winter you get all sorts of invitations to parties and dinners and you really get to see how Alaskans do it. We get together all the time in the winter. We share all the salmon, halibut, crab, deer, moose, caribou, bear, and anything else we may have harvested throughout the year. Spaghetti and moose balls simply rocks!

We also tell stories, also known as lies! Play cards and drink. Usually way too much of the latter! Then we go home and sleep. Sleep until the phone rings the next morning. Keep in mind the phone will only ring the next morning if you and your buddy have each finished at least half a bottle of scotch and two bottles of red wine! Can you say hurting units? I knew you could!

The phone is ringing to inform you that it is time to get your sorry, hung over ass out of bed for a beach picnic. The person on the other end, usually your friend's wife, shows no mercy on you or your friend. The only viable excuse for missing a beach picnic is death. Try as you may to argue that you really are near death from the preceding night's festivities this will only insure that they drive over to get you! You are going, deal with it!

Don't forget that all of this takes place in the winter! As a matter of fact, the only times I have ever received this wonderful call it was snowing sideways! Oh yeah! The wind is blowing at least thirty knots and whiteout conditions exist!

Beautiful day for an outing!

We always manage to build the fire right at the edge of the beach, just under the canopy. Somehow, someway the wind never seems to blow in that exact spot. It's actually warm around the fire! The fresh air seems to make your headache go away.

Someone sneaks off into the woods and comes back with enough freshly cut Alder or Willow sticks so everyone can enjoy "steak on a stick". "Steak on a stick" is the best! You simply use any steak you have deer, moose, caribou, or whatever and run your sharpened stick through and grill!

Game on an open fire is the best!

What do you know you have just experienced another great day in the Great Land!

Oh, don't forget to apologize to your friend's wife for all the bad things you called her when that damn phone rang!

That ain't a pigeon...

Every year in November we try to make it up to Haines for the Bald Eagle Festival. It usually runs the first or second week in November and is truly something to behold. It also can be one of the last fishing trips of the year.

There is a real late Chum Salmon run up the Chilkat River that attracts all of the eagles from everywhere. And I do mean everywhere! It is quite normal for there to be over 3000 eagles on that river at that time.

Sunrise in Haines.

It is truly hard to describe what it is like to see that many eagles in one place. There are ten or fifteen in every tree! Have you ever seen a flock of seagulls, no not that terrible band from the 80's, a real big flock of seagulls, well just imagine that they are all eagles! It really must be added to your life list! It is one of the natural wonders of the world.

They are all there for one last feast before the winter really sets in. Oh yeah...it's suppertime! The scene would make Caligula proud! There is gorging on Chum Salmon happening everywhere! And what a beautiful place for a final supper, the Chilkat valley.

Where's the Chum?

The young eagles grab a salmon and start going to town on it when five mature eagles will swoop in and take it away. You can literally hear the flesh being ripped from the fish and the swoosh of the eagles wings as they fly by. If you have not figured it out yet the eagles are not off in the distance, all of this is happening all around you. We are talking twenty feet away! Don't forget your camera and lot's of film or memory cards!

I know I said this was the last fishing trip of the year, but who cares if you don't catch anything with all of this happening. I think that is why it is called "fishing" and not "catching". Sometimes the value is in the experience!

Speaking of experiences, there is another facet to this trip that you may be fortunate enough to encounter. Do you know how angry you become when you have just washed your beautiful car and come out to find that a pigeon has left his calling card right in the middle of your shiny hood? Well, just try to imagine the size of the calling card an eagle leaves on your shiny hood! It tends to cover the entire hood and both fenders! And it doesn't just wash off either! Oh no…it's putty knife time!

I've heard it many times, "Dude, that ain't no pigeon!" But who cares, it's probably a rental car if you are in Haines.

The Haines Bald Eagle Festival is a must! There's good people, good food, and good beer to be had by all! Besides you really have not lived until you have been shat upon by an eagle!

I'll get your car too!

We three Kings...

Oh no! Our nephew Zac returns! This time his mother and father, Margie and Hoot Keely come along for the ride. It's a family fishing vacation, what more could you want? I firmly believe that the family that slays together stays together!

As much as I love to catch fish, and I really do love to catch fish! I think I love to help people catch fish even more! There's truly nothing like it.

It was another beautiful evening in Southeast so why not go fishing. We launched the boat in Auke Bay and headed out to the fishing grounds. Not too long a run since the Kings are supposed to be in thick this time of year. By the way it is June.

We drop the lines in the water, in the usual manner, and start to troll. Hoot and Cindy start telling stories about growing up in Oklahoma when one of the rods takes off!

Zac, big surprise, grabs the rod and the battle begins! The fish runs on him a couple of times and finally we land the mighty King Salmon! The skunk is off the boat! Zac starts his victory speech, but that will have to wait because another line just took off!

Now it is Hoot's turn. He takes the pole and starts to work the fish in. This fish is a little livelier than Zac's. He runs several times, and each time Hoot's smile gets a little bigger! Just about the time I think his face is going to break from smiling we land the fish! High fives all around!

The lines go back in the drink and Zac makes sure everyone on board knows his fish is the biggest!

More stories and the sun finally starts to fade when another rod pops out of the downrigger.

Now it's Margie's shot at glory. This is the best fish of the night for me. She listens to my every word as I coach her on landing this fish. Every time that fish ran her eyes got a little bigger. By the time we landed it her eyes were like saucers! She was so excited! And so was I!

Three Kings in one night, it just does not get better than that!

Three of a kind!

The next day it was back out to the old fishing grounds to see if our luck would hold out. Well the fishing was a lot slower that day. We only were able to convince one King to commit suicide.

A woman and her King!

We caught up on all the family gossip, besides any time you are able to catch even one King Salmon it is a great day!

The next day the weather was "iffy" at best so we decided to do a little flat fishing. We headed out just past Vanderbilt Reef and anchored up on a nice hump.

The lines went down and the action was pretty slow. But then again halibut fishing can be that way.

Then the bite started to come on. First Zac got a few nibbles and then Hoot started getting a few but neither one could seem to hook one.

They were getting quite tired of doing bait checks when Zac's rod took off!

This halibut had no intention of coming to the top! He fought and ran and shook like there was no tomorrow. The way Zac was straining and the way that rod was doubled over I just knew we had a "barn door" on the line!

Barn door?

Hoot and Zac passed the rod off several times trying to land the monster! Both working so hard there were veins on top of veins popping out!

Definitely a barn door!

I just knew we had at least a 300 pounder! Then I caught the first glimpse of the beast as if it were a ghost coming up from the deep. But there was a problem! It didn't look like a barn door! It looked like a ping pong paddle! And what was that chain doing in the picture?

Oh great! They have just brought up the anchor! No wonder it never ran. It must have twisted around the anchor during the fight. I can see now why that fish fought so hard, he was getting it from both ends!

Two ping pong paddles and one big anchor!

Well at least they did get to see a halibut and we get to hassle Zac about catching an anchor for the rest of his life!

Nothing like a hut in the woods...

For our summer vacation we thought it would be nice to take a road trip. See a little more of Alaska and drop our lines in a few new streams and lakes. So we loaded up the truck and got on the ferry for Haines.

We knew there was a Sockeye Salmon run there in July and we just couldn't wait to give it a try. Due to the time of year and the fact we were taking the dogs with us on this trip our lodging options were, shall we say limited. We had booked a cabin at this guest cabin operation, sight unseen and prepaid, and it was a very special place!

Each cabin was about 10x10 and the beds were basically a sheet of plywood on four 2x4 legs with a little two inch piece of foam rubber for a mattress. This became affectionately known as "The Hut".

Cozy!

Don't get me wrong, "The Hut" sucked! There is no way it could have been better or worse! Or so we thought!

Yes it could indeed be worse! The day before the trip Cindy started to get a cold. That made it much worse!

As I have mentioned before she loves to fish and there was no way this trip was going to be postponed. It's time to fish lets go!

Lutak dreams.

Besides we only had to stay in "The Hut" when it was time to sleep. The rest of the time we would be fishing. And we had only paid for three nights, we can put up with anything for three little nights! Right?

Cindy was miserable but we went fishing anyway. This was not your normal river fishing. No calm water here! It was rushing water, flip your spoon out there and try to piss off a salmon enough to bite kind of fishing!

Where's the Sockeye?

Oh did I mention that there were HUGE bear piles everywhere! Not exactly a relaxing day of fishing! But man was it fun!

The only thing I could seem to catch was trees and rocks. I picked up a few Dolly Varden but I was not fishing for Dolly Varden was I!

Another Dolly!

Cindy on the other hand was catching Sockeye left and right! It was actually a lot of fun just watching her catch so many fish.

She would hook into one and it would run upstream then turn and run downstream at a breakneck pace and she would be reeling like a mad woman!

Who cared that we were both getting quite the sunburn and eaten alive by No-See-Ums! When we were fishing she didn't even remember that she was sick. By 3 o'clock though she remembered and was exhausted so it was back to "The Hut" for a nap.

As you can probably guess, when you are sick the last thing you want to sleep on is plywood! This did not work very well at all. She tossed and turned for a couple of hours and we finally decided to go get a bite to eat.

On the way back to "The Hut" we employed a new plan; we stopped at the Haines Brewing Company and picked up a growler for the night. Back at "The Hut" we finished the growler and both sleep through the night!

The next morning we both felt like someone had beat the tar out of us but it was time to go fishing so we did. We beat feet to the local fishing shop for more supplies. To say we went through a little bit of gear is very kind. Fifty bucks later we were ready for the fishing hole. How did I get out of there for fifty bucks? Well I'm a cheap bastard! I went straight to the discount bin and bought every spoon I could find for less than $2.00! Laugh if you will, we caught fish!

By now Cindy's cold was really kicking her good so we only made it to about noon. We went back to "The Hut" and she passed out. After dinner we killed another growler and tried to sleep.

The next morning I told Cindy, "I don't care if it is prepaid let's get the Hell out of Dodge!" She thanked me for my humanity and we hit the road for Tok!

The drive to Haines Junction from Haines is absolutely beautiful! You go through the Chilkat valley and climb up into the alpine. Once you get over the pass you are in Canada.

Canada has a very interesting method of road repair. They don't just reduce the amount of lanes and fix what needs to be repaired. They come in and completely destroy at least thirty miles of road at a time! This is not an exaggeration! From looking at the "road" you are on, one would not believe there had ever been a road there before! This is the way the road was from Haines Junction to Beaver Creek. We spent the night in Beaver Creek. A real bed did wonders for Cindy!

The next day we drove to Tok, Alaska. We saw a lot of streams that we really wanted to fish but my mighty fisherwoman just was not up to it so we refrained.

After another good nights sleep we hit the road to Chicken! This is another beautiful drive. Once again lots of places to fish and the scenery was simply gorgeous!

Chicken, Alaska is a very interesting place. It is basically a gift shop, a bar, and a café. There are not any restrooms, only out houses and on all of the out houses are the words, "Chicken Poop!" Since there was no place to stay we continued on to Dawson City.

The only way into Dawson is by ferry on the Yukon River. This is a huge river and this town is so full of history it is truly amazing. There are gold dredges everywhere and the old town is still intact. It is like stepping back in time.

Although we did not fish here we still had a great time. During the day we rented scooters and rode all over the place. That night we went to an old fashioned gambling hall. This was fun! We were up right from the start! I gave the cashier a C-note and she gave me back $150 Canadian. Gotta love that exchange rate! We tore it up that night and the next day we headed to Whitehorse.

Crossing the mighty Yukon River.

Another great drive, we saw moose and bears and some really great lakes. Cindy was turning the corner on her cold and we decided that she would hold out to fish in Atlin, British Columbia.

After a morning of shopping in Whitehorse we took off for Atlin. Why Atlin you ask? Well we have heard from a lot of our fly fishing buddies that this is the place to go. Just a few hours and we were there.

The information about Atlin turned out to be true! This place is awesome! We found a nice stream for our evening fish and jumped in!

Grayling was the fish of choice that night and there were plenty of them! In an hour and a half we picked up about twenty-five Grayling! The action was constant. They were not huge but on light gear they were a blast!

Atlin Rocks!

The next morning we went over to Lake Como and got into a little trout action.

MMM...Trout!

The Rainbows were huge! We are talking one to three pounders and the water was so clear it was easy to place the flies. This was definitely some great fishing!

Trout...trout...pretty little trout!

I decided to take a break from fishing and play a little fetch with our lab Remington. I threw a stick a few times and he did his job and retrieved it like a good boy. When I grew tired of this game I told him to go sit down and leave me alone. He was not ready to quit so I, as a joke, pointed to a small tree that was sticking out of the water about fifteen feet from shore and said, "Remington, get the stick!" I never thought he would! Well he tried. He dove in and next thing I knew he was half way up that tree trying to bring it to me! It took me a while to stop laughing but I finally got his attention and called him off! He is such a good boy!

The next morning we headed off to Skagway to catch the ferry back home. This was a terrific trip, one that I would highly recommend and one that we will do again with a little more fishing time planned.

The side of a barn...

We have always loved duck hunting. I can't think of a better way to spend a morning, after the prime fishing season of course, than getting up at 4am, hiking out to the old blind, throwing out the decoys, sitting in a mud puddle in the driving rain! It's just the best!

Actually it really is a lot of fun. There is nothing like watching the sun rise and the thrill of the first wave of ducks. The endorphins start poppin' and the blood gets to flowin'.

Speaking of blood flowin', after that first wave with a little luck you, I mean I get to play retriever. Man that water is cold!

You see we have never had a dog that was designed for duck hunting. We have always had Scotties. Scotties may be hell on badgers or rats but they are not great swimmers and they tend to chew the crap out of anything they get their mouths on! Duck burger is not on my menu!

So for years we have gone hunting and I have had to wade out and play retriever. I have always loved to watch a good dog work in the field. It is truly a thing of beauty. If you can't tell I have always been quite jealous of the other hunters and their dogs.

We had always been renters and it is just about impossible to find a place to rent with a big dog. But finally we bought a house. Now we can have a great hunting dog. Now I will get the opportunity to make someone else jealous with my brilliant beast. The time is now!

The first thing I did was buy the book "Water Dog" and I read it forwards and backwards. I had to learn everything I possibly could because I was going to have the greatest hunting dog the world had ever seen. He will be an absolute machine! Blind retrieves…multiple retrieves…hell he might even learn to pluck them on the way back to shore! He will be brilliant!

Then we bought the beast! He was an absolutely magnificent looking animal. Broad head, tight eyes, great stance, just about the most perfect black lab you have ever seen.

We named him Remington after an old shotgun that a friend gave us after a fishing trip a few years ago. That shotgun had a relief carving on the stock of a dog that looked very much like Remington. It's a tribute to a good friend, what can I say.

The work begins. Remington and I were never apart for more that three hours. I took him to work and walked and worked with him at every break and lunch for a year and a half.

He was house broken in less than a week. I'm telling you this dog truly is brilliant!

It was time for Rem's first hunt. I was so excited I could not sleep. I just knew he was going to be brilliant. All the other hunters were going to be jealous and I was not going to get wet for the first time ever! Oh happy day!

We woke up at 4am and loaded Rem up in the truck and headed out to the Mendenhall Wetlands for our hunt.

We hiked out to the blind and Cindy kept Rem on a lead while I set up the decoys. It was a glorious morning and he was performing in the blind like he had been there a thousand times before. He was brilliant!

I told him to lie down and he did. I told him to sit between us and he did. And when the first wave of ducks came he sat at attention and watched them like there was some sort of radar in his head that was locked and loaded.

They came in just right. It was like we were watching that Larry Czonka hunting show!

I sprang up and Bam…Bam…Bam! And the ducks all flew away! How the hell had I missed every single one of them?

I reloaded and the next wave came and Rem locked in and Bam…Bam…Bam! And they all flew away again!

Holy Crap! I was so focused on Rem's training I had forgotten to go to the range myself! I couldn't hit the side of a barn!

After a few more missed opportunities, through Cindy's snickering, I said let's bag this thing.

I looked down at Rem and he had this look in his eyes and yes I could read his mind. He was saying, "Pa…it's okay. I was going to retrieve the decoys anyway!"

Remington J. Birddog

Alms for the poor...

Cindy and I loaded up the boat for a normal day of fishing for King Salmon. What does this mean? Well we made sure the boat was full of gas. Put the bait on water to thaw. Put our Scottie, Monopoly, on board and packed our customary tuna sandwiches and pop.

For years my poor wife has caught a great deal of crap over the fact that we always seem to have tuna sandwiches on the boat. I don't know why it is such a bad thing to always have the same thing on board. We like tuna sandwiches and there is something to be said for consistency.

Anyway we decided to fish the Breadline on this fine day. We dropped in the lines and started to troll.

We trolled up and down the bread line for hours. I changed the gear and still there were not any hits of any kind. It was proving to be just one of those days. It was still a great day. It was much better than being at work even if the action was non-existent.

We decided we would troll on over to Lena Point. We had some friends tell us they had picked up a nice King over there just about a week prior. So we pointed the boat that way and had lunch.

The tuna sandwiches were good as always and we continued to fish without any change in the action.

As we were trolling we heard something odd. It sounded like people in need of assistance. We jumped up and started to look around to see where the voices were coming from and we spied a couple of kayaks that were coming up to the boat from behind.

Finally I could make out what they were saying, "Do you have any food? Do you have any food?"

And then I could see who it was making this strange request. It was three of our friends, who shall remain nameless. Why will they remain nameless? Well they are the three that had given Cindy the hardest time about the tuna and I refuse to make them famous. They know who they are and they are shamed enough!

They pulled up beside us and said they had gone out kayaking and remembered to bring the beer but forgot to bring any food!

We gave them the dreaded tuna sandwiches and they devoured them like barbarians! They also said that they were the best tuna sandwiches ever! I would have thought they would have tasted like crow! But I guess even crow tastes good if you are hungry enough!

We finished the day without any fish but to this day I can yell at a party, "Do you have any food?" and watch our friends turn red!

Can you say "barn door"...

My mother was in town for her annual fishing trip. She comes up just about every year and she expects to catch fish. If we don't catch fish there is definitely hell to pay. You see she calls herself "The Fisherchick" because that is what she loves to do. Her email address is "The Fisherchick", she signs letters "The Fisherchick", I think you get the picture.

Seeing me, her only child, is really secondary to the fishing. I'm not exaggerating! One year she came up and we couldn't seem to find a fish and I really thought she was going to disown me! It was brutal!

Anyway she was up but she was not going to be doing much of the fishing that year. She had just finished undergoing treatment for breast cancer and she was really quite weak. Her doctors prescribed this trip to boost her morale and, I firmly believe, to get her out of their hair for a few days.

We loaded up the boat for a day of halibut fishing, just my mother and I out on the sea with lots of time to catch up on things. I figured halibut fishing would be the easiest on her. We could just anchor up in a nice flat bay and relax. If we caught something it would just be a bonus.

The water was flat everywhere. It was truly one of those rare and glorious days in Southeast.

I decided to go try our luck in Barlow Cove so off we went. As we were cruising through North Pass I joked with mom that I had forgotten the gun and that meant we were destined to catch a monster. She laughed and we kept on cruising.

We ran about three quarters of the way into Barlow Cove before I decided to drop the anchor. I found a nice hump at about two hundred feet and we hooked up.

We threw lines in and ran them down to the bottom and started to chat. We had a great visit and were able to finish lunch before we were disturbed. Then we were really disturbed!

There were no bumps on the line, no signs at all of what was about to happen. One of the rods instantly doubled completely over under the boat!

I grabbed the rod and tried like hell to get it out of the rod holder! As I was doing this I noticed that the boat was starting to spin around on the anchor. I finally got the rod out and realized that this was no ordinary fish!

Mom grabbed her camcorder and started filming. She asked if she could help and I told her to just get it all on film. I knew she really could not do anything else anyway.

It was all I could do to get this fish off the bottom. It finally started to come up and I worked the rod in the usual fashion. You know…pull up…reel down…pull up…reel down.

I was able to get it about half the way up when it went on the first run. The rod doubled under the boat again, almost taking me with it and the reel screamed like a banshee on the way down!

I started talking to the fish at this point. "Oh shit! Stop fish stop! Please don't go all the way to the bottom!"

Well it did go all the way back down and I started bringing it back up again. By now I was starting to get pretty tired. I really did not want that fish to run again.

This time it was a little more willing to obey my desires. It kept on coming up. Past the half way point. Somewhere past the three quarter point it must have seen the boat and it ran again.

At this point I was totally soaked with sweat. I looked like I just got out of the shower. And my body was so pumped up I could barely use my arms. I begged the fish to please stop!

Somehow it did. It only went down about half way that time. So I started bringing it up again.

I knew that in my current physical state that I was only going to get one chance to land this beast. So I told mom to tie the end of the halibut harpoon to the cleat opposite of me and to get the spear ready. She did and she placed it right next to me. I told her that we were only going to have one shot at this fish and I was really going to need her to hold the rod when I gave it to her. She agreed and we got ready.

The fish surfaced about ten feet off the back of the boat and my mother shrieked! It was by far the largest fish either of us had ever seen. I've heard it said that big halibut look like a barn door and that is true! Until you have seen one up close and personal you really can't imagine it!

I pulled the fish up to the boat and handed her the rod. Just before I told her, "If it runs you drop the rod!" I grabbed the harpoon and thrust it into the side of the fish. The fish apparently did not approve of this action. It dove straight down, until it ran out of rope and started yanking the boat around in circles! My mother screamed that the fish was going to sink the boat! But the fish quickly tired and the boat steadied.

I pulled the fish back up to the side of the boat and ran another rope through its mouth and gills and tied it off to the side of the boat. Now is when I really needed the gun. They are so much more accommodating when you have the correct fire power. Halibut are much like third world countries in that respect.

Well I didn't have the gun so I would have to resort to popping a gill and letting it bleed out. Okay I beat the crap out of it with the baseball bat for good measure too.

Anyway after about an hour of bleeding and beating the fish seemed subdued enough to bring on board but I was not going to take any chances. Once in the boat I would hog tie the fish in the shape of a great big "U" so it could not hurt any one.

How was I going to get the fish in the boat you ask? Well fortunately halibut are very slimy and once you get them sliding in the boat there is no stopping them!

Once in the boat I quickly hog tied the fish and took a well deserved break. Then I remembered that I had to pull the anchor by hand. Wonderful. The very next day I bought an anchor pulling system. It really didn't seem that expensive anymore!

On the way back to the dock I called a friend to meet us there and assist. Trust me he got plenty of halibut!

Once we were able to get the fish in the back of the truck, some two hours after it had been bled out it started to rock back and forth in the bed.

For the record the fish weighed in at 174 pounds and I can promise you that we have not forgotten the gun again!

That's a barn door!

Barn door II...

Well if there is one thing I have learned over the years about fishing it is this; if I happen to catch the biggest fish of my life within two weeks my wife will catch one bigger. It's the cruel hard truth. The fish gods have to keep me down and Cindy simply must keep me in my place.

Having said that, we had been trying to get out to Icy Straits to do a little halibut fishing for several days but the water just would not allow. It was Sunday and our last chance for another week so we filled up the boat and gave it hell one more time.

You see getting to Icy Straits from Juneau can be a bugger. It's either get the crap beat out of you on the way there only to find that it is worse there or get the crap beat out of you on the way back. It's pretty rare that you get a nice trip both ways.

The water that day was pretty rough but we decided to burn the fuel and run on out to Couverden and see if it was any better after that big right turn.

You guessed it, it was not. So we turned and ran back to North Pass with our tail between our legs.

As we were running we noticed that the water was improving. The sky was still gray but the water was definitely getting better. Maybe all is not lost.

We decided to drop anchor there in North Pass and at least fish until it did start to kick up.

So we found our spot in about two hundred feet of water and dropped the lines. There was a slight mist so we donned our trusty rain gear and kicked back to shoot the breeze.

About thirty minutes into this venture Cindy started getting a bite. She went back to her rod and started to work the bait and got a nice strike.

We could tell it was not a huge fish but it was a nice one just the same. Without too much difficulty she landed a decent fifty pound halibut. Alright the skunk is off the boat and all that fuel we burned is now paid for.

Since the water was still cooperating she ran her line back down. She bounced her bait on the bottom a couple of times and the freight train hit!

She yelled that she might need a little help and I turned around to see her rod bent all the way under the boat and the veins popping out of her neck! So I went back to assist.

I told her that she needed to catch that fish and she agreed. I strapped a fighting belt on her and helped get the rod in the belt then I brought up the other line and started getting the harpoon ready.

Somehow my little 5'3" one hundred and twenty pound wife had coaxed that monster to start coming up. I just coached her. Pull up...reel down...pull up...reel down. Besides I knew once that fish started up to touch that pole was certain death! She is after all an Alaskan girl and Alaskan girls kick ass!

She got the fish up about half way when it decided it didn't want to go up anymore and that reel screamed just like a banshee just like my reel had done just two weeks prior. Damn it she is going to catch a bigger fish I just know it!

The fish stopped, you guessed it, on the bottom and she had to start all over again. She was now more determined than ever. This fish is going in the freezer!

She got it turned around again and this time it seemed to want to come up. At the halfway mark it was still rising steadily. Same at the three quarter mark. There was no turning back now in Cindy's mind!

Then it broke the surface about six feet off the back of the boat and I was shocked! Not only was this fish bigger than mine, it was scary big!

I told her to bring it over a little closer so I could use the harpoon and she did but when I tried to drive the spear through the fish I hit bone and this really pissed off the beast! It dove down a good fifty feet and I swear the look I received at that very moment, well, let's just say that I no longer fear death!

Cindy brought the beast up again and this time I didn't miss. What a relief! The fish was ours!

I pulled out the hand held thunder stick and dispatched the monster post haste! This part was much better than the way I had to deal with the fish I caught two weeks ago.

We decided that we were done fishing for the day so I pulled the beast into the boat and quickly hog tied it, just to be safe and we headed for the dock. Once again I called a friend to meet us at the dock for assistance.

We headed for the house and discovered that the fish was quite a bit larger than mine. It weighed in at 214 pounds!

We spent the next few hours processing the fish and were pretty much at the point of exhaustion when we realized that we still had a fifty pounder to deal with too! Gee what a problem to have, too many halibut to clean! I'll take it everyday!

We have since decided that we have caught all of the barn doors we intend to bring home. If we are fortunate enough to hook into another one we will bring it up, snap a picture, and cut the line! They are way too much work but they are way too much fun!

Cindy described what it is like to catch one of these monsters best. She said, "It's like having someone roll you up in a blanket and then beat the crap out of you with a pool cue for, say, two hours!"

I was so proud of Cindy. She took that fish from bottom to freezer all by herself!

Okay it's bigger than mine!

Funter bay dreams...

We had heard a rumor of King's being caught out at Lizard Head Reef so we thought we would give it a shot. Lizard Head is out past Funter Bay on Admiralty Island. It's a pretty good run out there so we thought we would maximize our fuel usage and just spend the night in Funter Bay and fish two days there.

We made the long run and started to fish. It was an absolutely gorgeous day, no wind and skies so blue it was like looking into a giant ice cave.

Good thing the weather was nice because the fishing was, well, fishing. I tried everything I could think of to entice a King to strike! We ran cut plugs, whole herring, hoochies, you name it we tried it that day.

We did see a couple of other boats pick up a King but I guess it just was not our day. Oh well, it happens! We will give it hell tomorrow!

So we pulled into Funter Bay to spend the night. Funter Bay is the kind of place that is Alaska. Not only is it a beautiful completely protected harbor but it is chock full of history. At one point there was a canary located there, only ruins remain today and it was also the location of one of the internment camps used during WWII.

Today there are a handful of cabins and lodges that are located there and a nice free floating dock for adventurous sorts like us to tie up to when there is room. On this night there were only four other boats tied up in the whole bay.

We tied up to the dock and started preparing for our cookout. We came prepared for the possibility that fresh fish might not be on the menu. Although being prepared is not all that necessary in Funter Bay because on the dock is a sign that instructs boaters what VHF channel to call on and fresh dungie's will be brought right out to you for a fee of $5.00 each!

The steaks were great and the beer was cold and the view was amazing. The sunset came around 10pm and the sky was filled with reds, pinks, yellows, and silver shimmering like the light tends to do on the side of a five pound rainbow trout!

Oh did I mention the whales? We could hear humpback whales playing in the surf off in the distance. And occasionally their spouts would rise off the horizon like distant smoke signals telling us this is Alaska.

Now for the sleeping accommodations, at the time we had a 19ft aluminum boat with a canvas enclosure. No beds!

It was not really designed for sleeping. Cindy slept on the floor across the bow in a "V" shape and I slept on the floor between the seats with our Scottie, Monopoly, sleeping on my chest! Very restful!

The next morning the weather had turned on us somewhat. The sky was gray and a fine mist filled the air. Cindy whipped up a quick breakfast and Monopoly pooped on the dock and we decided it would be best to run on back in just in case the weather really decided to kick up.

As we were getting the boat ready to run we started hearing this really strange sound coming from just outside the bay. It sounded like the world's largest can of pop being opened followed by a splashing sound. We decided we would investigate on the way out.

We pulled out of the bay and saw what we had been hearing. It was a huge group of humpback whales bubble feeding. It was amazing! They would all dive down and then a huge ring of bubbles would appear on the surface and then the herring would start to boil out of the water and boom! Seven or eight whales would come up out of the water with their mouths wide open completely full of herring! We watched this over and over again for about twenty minutes then we turned tail and ran for home.

Bubble feeding Humpbacks.

That evening and that morning were simply the best! Once again it's all about the experience not necessarily the catching. But sometimes it is about the catching!

On the way back in we stopped at North Pass and threw the lines over for halibut. After about an hour Cindy picked up a nice sixty pound halibut and Monopoly was thrilled!

Nice Butt!

I've mentioned before that she loved to lick fish when they came on board, well, she licked that fish from head to tail and that was the day she became known as our little "Halimutt"! She smelled awful! And every hair on that dog was completely stiff like she had been dipped in halibut mousse and styled by some deranged Hollywood hairdresser!

But she was happy and so were we! There is nothing better than a "Halimutt" on board! Ah the sweet smell of success!

Cindy's got a big old butt...

It was another one of those days when the water was as flat as a frog pond. The sun shining off the water bright and warm and lines were already on the bottom. What more could you ask for?

We were in North Pass along with about ten other boats and a huge group of humpback whales. North Pass is a favorite feeding ground for humpbacks. Almost any day of the week you can run into North Pass and find whales spouting and feeding. There is nothing like being anchored up and having one of these graceful beasts come right up beside the boat and take a look at you. I wonder if they are thinking, "Hmmm...must taste like chicken!"

Just sayin' howdy!

On days like this Cindy and I love to halibut fish. It's so relaxing to bob up and down in the boat. Usually after lunch we take turns napping in the boat. One gets to sleep and the other one has to watch the rods. That is if they can stay awake!

Well it was one of those glorious days. Cindy had been asleep for about an hour and I was watching the rods, wink wink, when her rod took off! Nothing like being yanked from an all relaxing sun nap by the sound of a halibut rod banging up and down in a rod holder!

She grabbed the rod and we knew instantly that she had hooked into a nice halibut. The rod doubled over and the reel screamed every time that fish ran! I got the halibut spear ready and she kept on working that fish to the top.

The fish surfaced and she brought it over to the side of the boat for me. Just as I got ready to spear the fish her line snapped and whizzed right past my head and everything went into slow motion! The fish just froze there at the top as if it did not realize it was free and I quickly thrust the spear into the fish. It was ours! It didn't get away!

I pulled out the gun and shot it, just for good measure, and all of the other boats started to whoop and holler! When you hear a gunshot from a boat that is halibut fishing you know a big one has just come on board. Once we got it in the boat we figured out it weighed about ninety pounds and would keep us full of fish and chips for quite a while.

The one that DIDN'T get away!

Then it was back to the more important business of the day, sleep! We both dozed off for another good hour and why not? The skunk was definitely off of our boat! Cindy's big butt proved that!

Crab cruise time...

We have this really good friend named Mary Lehman. She is an absolute sweetheart of a person and a riot to boot! She and her husband Stan moved here a few years ago from

Wisconsin so as you may have guessed everything Alaskan just blows her mind.

She is afraid of just about everything we do. She thinks we are all crazy! Hunting scares her. Fishing scares her. Boating scares her. Hell the way we like to pour fresh crab out on a picnic table after it's cooked and dig in with our hands has permanently scarred her! All she kept saying was, "Where's the drawn butter? Where's the utensils? Where's the humanity?" She will not have anything to do with crab after that experience! Or so we thought!

One of her daughters was coming up for a visit with her boyfriend so Mary asked if I would be willing to take them out in our boat one evening. I agreed and suggested that we could pull a crab pot or two and give them a real Alaskan experience. But I insisted that she come along too. I was already scheming at that point! She agreed and we made it a date.

Cindy and I set the pots a couple of day's prior out at Eagle Beach. And the plans were set.

On the night of the "Crab Cruise" we all met at the boat launch out at Amlaga Harbor. Cindy and I half expected Mary not to show or if she did show we expected her to show up in a full Gumby suit! Well she made it and all she had to keep her afloat was a bright yellow Mustang Float coat.

There was terror in her eyes! She was facing her fears and we were proud of her. The five of us took off for Eagle Beach.

Normally when we pull the pots Cindy and I simply put the legal crab in the live well or if we are going right back in we throw them into a burlap bag. Nice and clean, no mess. But tonight I wanted to give these rookies the whole crab experience! Instead of putting them neatly away I just tossed them on the deck and let them run wild! There were crabs everywhere! You could not get away from them! Those of you that don't know, Dungies are quite mobile out of the water. And if you happen to have an issue with arachnophobia you better watch out!

One crawled up Mary's extra tuff boot and she freaked out! Her eyes became like saucers and her face went pale as a ghost. Then our dear sweet Mary became possessed. She started screaming in some language that is not of this earth! I started looking for the four horsemen of the apocalypse! I thought Linda Blair was in our boat! The only thing missing was the pea soup!

A mess of crab!

I pulled the crab off of her and tried to steady her nerves and we all laughed for at least twenty minutes. We laughed so hard we all started to cry. It was absolutely the funniest thing I have ever seen!

Mary was not amused. When I told her how we usually deal with crab I thought she was going to have me drawn and quartered. She was so mad. But I think that made it even better!

After we all stopped laughing/crying we headed over to Poundstone Rock for a little wildlife viewing. We watched the sea lions play on the buoy for a little while. Sea lions are always on that buoy by the way. Then we shot on into North Pass to try and catch a whale or two.

We could see the whales spouting in the distance but it was too far to run that night so we thought we had to settle for watching a Bald Eagle doing a little fishing from the shore.

Just then a massive humpback whale surfaced right in front of the boat and I had to shut it down in a hurry. We spun the boat around and were treated to a wonderful up close whale encounter. What a treat!

A few weeks after this wonderful evening we were informed that every time one of her relatives comes up we had to take them out on a "Crab Cruise". The events of that evening were all her daughter talked about apparently. We agreed and have since made the "Crab Cruise" a must for anyone that comes up to visit.

Mary's crab!

Oh by the way, yes Mary is still talking to us! We love our Mary and I guarantee you would too! But she still won't eat crab!

A nice diversion...

Sometimes one simply gets tired of smelling like herring and fish guts. Sometimes the roar of a motor, even a four stroke is just too much. Sometimes you just want to completely immerse yourself in the beauty of the day and truly live "right here right now". On days like this Cindy and I try to go kayaking.

There is nothing more relaxing than gently gliding through the surf with a light breeze in your face and the feeling of your oneness with nature. Especially after the Hell that you've just gone through lugging your kayak down to the water! Kayaks ain't light!

Kayaks also require a great deal of skill to maneuver in a safe manner. Oh yeah, they look really easy to operate from shore but sit your fat out of shape ass down in one and you are ready for a real workout!

Kayak boy!

First you have to spend about a half hour figuring out how to get in the damn thing. If you are too close to shore you get stuck on bottom and if you are too far from shore your boots fill up.

Then you get to spend another few minutes getting used to the constant fear of rolling it over. Why is this a constant fear? Well every time you breathe the boat yanks one way or the other and you know that if you do happen to roll over hypothermia will set in so quick you will be a goner before you know it.

Anyway now you start to get comfortable with the whole idea and the boat actually starts to go in the direction you desire when all of a sudden there is the coldest sensation you have ever experienced in of all places your armpit! That wonderful 42 degree water that is the Pacific Ocean has just run down your paddle, down your sleeve, and soaked your steaming armpit. So this is how you learn not to raise your paddle too high. Okay I get it now!

We have chosen the Fritz Cove area for this adventure. There are a few islands in that area and we intend to explore them all before sundown.

We paddled around a couple of them and found a nice one with a nice beach for lunch. After the kayaks are hauled up on the beach, you would not want your ride home to drift away would you? We had lunch. After our usual lunch of tuna sandwiches we decided to explore the island. There are some great spots for camping and we decided we would have to do just that one day but for now we better get going. By the way, sex on one of these deserted islands is simply wonderful! We highly recommend this addition to the adventure.

Beach fun!

As we were leaving the island a group of dolphins decided to join us. This was awesome! They swam all around the kayaks. They went under us, beside us, and even stopped and took a look at us. This was really a cool experience. Ah nature.

We continued on our circumnavigation of Spuhn Island. We made our way all the way back around to Fritz Cove when we were joined by a group of seals. They were quite curious and popped their little heads up within ten feet of our kayaks. Cindy has always described seals by saying their heads look like milk bottles floating on the waves. "Look there is another milk bottle" she often says.

Anyway they became bored with us and moved on and we concluded our wonderful adventure by lugging those damn kayaks back up the beach to the car.

Here is the best part of our little kayaking diversion, the next morning neither of us could move! We were so sore it was pathetic. Kayaking is not for old fat people! You have all now been warned! But it was worth every ache and pain.

Mom's forty pounder...

As I have said before my mother loves to fish. She really only comes up here to catch something big and slimy. Seeing me is just a dirty necessity. Fishing is the whole reason for the trip.

And if for some reason I am not able to find her a fish there truly is Hell to pay! She gets grumpy and nasty and sometimes resorts to playing the guilt card. "I'm just your mother. I may never get to come up here again. It's okay... sniff sniff...just seeing you is enough for me." Yeah right! It works but she is still full of crap!

Well she came up near the end of June and wanted to catch a King Salmon so we fished like crazy! There is a period right at the end of June until the middle of July when the King's drop off and the Silvers have just not arrived so it can be a little slow trolling. We hit it hard that first weekend and no luck. Not even a bump, just hours and hours of dragging herring and listening to her whine.

We tried to go halibut fishing but she was not interested. She wanted a King and by God she was going to have one! I think she was starting to question my fishermanhood!

We decided to go on an evening fish right after work on Wednesday of that week just to get her off of our backs.

The evening was absolutely beautiful. The sun was shining and the sky was clear and blue. We dropped in at the North Douglas boat launch so we could fish the False Outer Point area. There were just a handful of boats in the area so the trolling was easy.

We had dinner and picked up a couple of Tom Cod. Not exactly what we were shooting for but better than nothing, I guess.

The sun was just starting to set over the Chilkat's and the sky turned a vivid red, pink, silver, and blue just like a Machatanz painting. And the stress of our workday had all but left when a rod started screaming!

I grabbed the pole and set the hook and quickly gave it to Mom. Like I had any choice in the matter. She was on that rod like a bear on a gut pile!

The King broke the surface about fifteen feet from the boat and ran straight at the stern. Mom screamed, "Oh my God it's huge!" She was right! It was like that scene in the movie Jaws when the police chief said, "We need a bigger boat"!

The fish dove under the boat and she announced that the line was slack and that she had lost the fish. I grabbed the pole and reeled like my right wrist and hand had been replaced with a Kitchenaid mixer! There was no way that fish was going to be lost; I just could not deal with that bowl of guilt. The line was slack because it was running right at the boat again. Somehow I was able to catch up to the fish and get it to turn.

At that very second the pole was once again yanked from my hands! And the fight was going to begin in earnest.

Here is the best part of this whole story for me. For the next thirty minutes I got to tell my mother to "shut up and reel! No I said shut up! Reel! Do as I say!" Ah the worm had turned!

The fish finally tired and we were able to land the mighty beast. Once on board I was shocked to find out that it weighed in at forty pounds! That's a huge fish for this area!

The Fisherchick is victorious!

Well my inheritance was secured for yet another year! And somehow she did not remember all of that "shut up" business! Ah life is good! Mom loves me!

Chummin' for bait...

Not having a boat is no reason to fore go fishing here in Juneau. We have spent many a night down at the Dipac dock throwin' pixies at slimy old Chum.

Dipac is short for the Douglas Island Pink and Chum hatchery. It is really something to see when you are here in Juneau. They not only raise and release Pink and Chum, they also raise and release King and Silver Salmon.

When the fish are running it is truly an amazing place. The water literally boils with fish. One fish at the far end will get spooked and all of his comrades just take off! It's like doing "The Wave" at a football game but much better! Thousands of fish all freakin' out at the same time, what a rush.

A lot of locals go down to the hatchery just to get crab bait. They will give you just about all the carcasses you can haul off but what fun is that? If you are going to go to the trouble of driving there you might as well get a hook wet. Besides television in the summertime sucks anyway.

The fish are so thick you are just about guaranteed to catch a ton of fish in an evening. Just flip that pixie and let the fight begin.

Believe it or not a slimy old green Chum can put up a pretty good fight. Especially if he is hooked in the tail! Oh did I mention its okay to snag in that area? You are just going to catch and release anyway so why not enjoy? But bring plenty of pixies cause you are going to lose quite a few. But when you go home when the sun sets at 10pm and your arms are aching from fighting fish it will all be worth the $15 you spent on pixies.

It's also fun to watch the fish on what we call the Final Tour! What is the Final Tour? Well those are the fish that pretty much resemble Keith Richards these days. Mangled... parts falling off...but still dead set on getting some action! If you know what I mean! There is nothing more pathetic than an old decrepit dude cruising the local bar tryin' to score! Oh well, guys will be guys.

Chum fun!

Oh one other thing that is important to remember, bring your kids! Bring your neighbor's kids or just someone that has never been fishing and I guarantee you will have a fishing partner for the rest of the season!

J. KEVIN CURRY

Loaded for bear...

Well it was time to get serious about a bear hunt. So my good friend Jerry Dana and I started the planning.

Bear hunting is not something to be taken lightly. There is an old saying here in Alaska that goes, "Sometimes you get the bear and sometimes the bear gets you!" Not the most reassuring of sayings but very true just the same.

Anyway we planned our trip all winter long and when the spring came we were ready for Yogi. We loaded up the boat for a good ten day hunt. Plenty of good food, wine, beer, scotch and enough fire power to take out a small country! Oh yeah, we could have whipped the Middle Eastern country of Chad's ass!

We blasted off for St. James Bay to begin our hunt and our wives were feeling pretty good about the prospects of being rid of us for the next ten days. Good for them they deserved a break!

Well we pulled into St. James Bay and anchored up and what do you know, there's Yogi just a walkin' down the beach. We quickly made our way to shore and dispatched that bruin with heavenly force!

He was not a huge bear by any standards but he was my first bear and he was beautiful! An absolutely perfect hide with no rub marks at all. I firmly believe he woke up that morning from his long winter nap…stretched…and bam!

I called Cindy to tell her the good news. When she answered the phone I said "Bear down" and she started screaming at me! She did not understand what I was saying; she thought I couldn't hear her so she was yelling into the phone. It just did not make any sense to her that we could possibly have a bear already.

I finally was able to convince her that we really had a bear and told her to meet us at the dock in about four hours.

We got that sucker skinned out and beat feet for home. When we got to the dock we tied the carcass to a pole and carried it up the dock on our shoulders. If you have never seen a skinned bear, well, it looks pretty much like a skinned dude! Yeah you could say we got some pretty good looks coming up that dock. One old lady finally asked the question everyone else was afraid to ask, "What the Hell is that?" And I responded, "Oh it's just Tom…just kidding!"

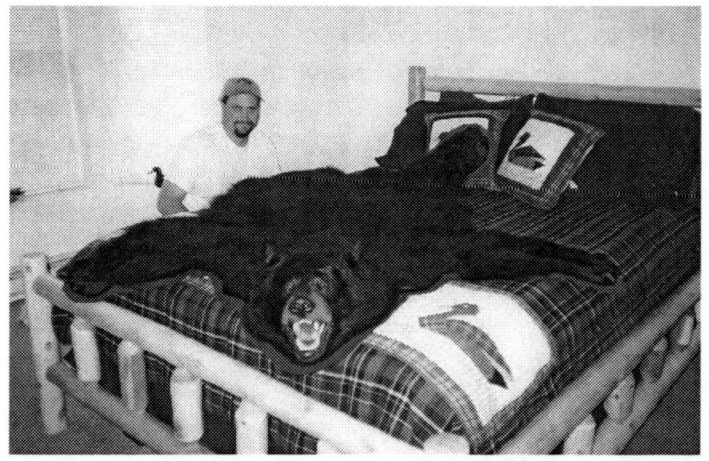

Yogi in the house!

What a wonderful experience and yes I know my next bear hunt will not be so easy. My wife is still upset about getting ripped out of her ten day break from me but she does love the way that bear looks on the wall. Every time we go into a house that is the first thing she looks for…a place for our bear rug! By the way…bear burgers on the bar-b-que rock!

Katie water...

As you can guess by now we have a lot of really good friends that love to fish. Ed and Catalina Haney are two more.

Ed is a retired Navy guy so bad water really does not affect him very much. He will fish just about anything. Six foot...eight foot...ten foot seas, no problem! The rougher the better, it really does not seem to matter. And the part that really gets me is he catches fish, a lot of fish.

Now Katie on the other hand only likes to go when the water is a frog pond. Ed once took her out in ten foot seas and I don't think she has forgiven him for it yet. By the way it is okay to be a fair-weather fisherman. It's better to fish with someone you love than...wait a minute...fishing with someone you hate is still fishing so never mind!

Anyway any time we see flat water we call it "Katie water". Enough said.

Katie water!!!

Cindy and I had been raving on and on about how good the halibut fishing was out in Icy Straits and I think Ed was sick of hearing about it so he invited us to go fishing with them and we would make the run all the way out there if the weather permitted.

The date was set and that morning the sun was shining and the water was shimmering like the light tends to do off of the scales of a freshly dispatched King Salmon. It was "Katie water" and life was good!

We loaded up the boat and made the run out to Icy Strait. About half way there the water started to kick up just a bit but Ed decided it was just a tidal thing so we proceeded.

When we arrived there were a few other boats on the old hump ahead of us but there was still plenty of room.

All of the lines went in the drink at about the same time. Cindy hit the bottom first and bumped the bait a couple of times and boom! She started bringing up the first halibut of the day. It was a ping pong paddle, about fifteen pounds but who cares.

Then I hit bottom and bounced a few times then up came another ping pong paddle.

Cindy's turn again. It was Déjà vu all over again.

We started shaking them off and waiting for one with a little more girth.

Cindy would bring one up then I would bring one up. Then Cindy, then me…I think you get the picture.

Ed's frustration is becoming palatable. He is a competitor as most fishermen are and he was not liking that action. Finally he suggests that we run over behind this little island in the distance and anchor up for lunch. Cindy and I have three on board so what the heck!

We anchor up and throw out the lines for good measure and have a wonderful lunch. Ed is starting to relax and have fun again when my rod takes off.

This was a much better fish. And Ed was a good sport and helped me land a nice forty pounder.

I of course have to rub it in and announce that Cindy and I are done for the day. We have limited out! Ed grumbled... "Let's go home".

Up comes the anchor and we are headed for home. Once back at the house Ed let me know that those fish did not count toward my yearly total since they were caught on his boat. I agreed and we all had a good laugh. We split the fish with him like a good Alaskan would do and celebrated yet another great day in the Great Land.

Ed is a good sport!

The fisherchick kicks some butt...

My mom, the fisherchick, was back in town for another visit and in the mood to do a little bottom feeding. Finally, she never wants to halibut fish. I think she just likes to watch me work. Somehow she must be getting even with me for my childhood. Oh well, I will take it when I can get it.

The sun was shining and the weather was unusually warm for the Juneau area and the water was most definitely "Katie water". Flat flat flat you just gotta love that! So we blasted over to St. James Bay so I could show Mom where I had bagged a nice black bear earlier that spring. We were actually planning on fishing out at Vanderbilt Reef but the weather was just too nice not to take advantage of the situation.

I showed her the beach where Yogi was dispatched with heavenly force and we threw the lines in just on a whim. No anchor this time. Just a little drift fish while we enjoyed the sun. Life is good!

The good life!

After about twenty minutes of slowly bumping along the bottom Mom got a hit. She was so excited.

That fish jerked and ran and fought and she was smiling from ear to ear.

When it finally made its ghostlike appearance, their white bellies shimmer in the water very much like a poltergeist coming up from the deep, she started screaming, "It's a halibut! It's a halibut!"

It sure was a halibut. Not a monster but a nice size fish for her first ever halibut. She was thrilled!

The fisherchick and her butt!

We then decided to run on over to Vanderbilt Reef and try our luck. It's just a quick fifteen minute run from St. James Bay besides we already had the skunk off of the boat.

We anchored up in about 180 feet of water and threw the lines in the drink. Ah it was finally time to relax and have a little lunch.

The tuna sandwiches were exquisite and any breeze that was there completely went away. It was downright hot and we were all becoming very sleepy. Time for a halibut nap…well maybe not!

My rod doubled completely over without any warning and the boat yanked to the right. I struggled to free the rod from the holder and the fight was on! This fish did have some size to it and a whole lot of piss and vinegar to boot! She was not happy about the surprise in the middle of that free lunch she had found.

I started working her up from the bottom and every time I would get her about to the one hundred foot level she would say "No thank you" and shoot back down to the bottom. She did this four times and I was starting to get pretty tired.

Finally she decided to cooperate and I brought her on up. Cindy harpooned her and she was ours! This one was definitely a shooter so I grabbed the gun and whacked her in true Soprano style!

Mom freaked out! She did not know that this was the correct procedure for dealing with large halibut. Oh well Mom your son is a killer. Deal with it!

Butts on the boat!

Yet another day of great fishing action in Southeast Alaska. Mom had her first halibut and I had a one hundred pounder.

Passin' the time away...

As you may have guessed by now winters here in the Great Land are long and dark. The company of good friends and the occasional sun break to Hawaii, Mexico, or Vegas are the only things that get you through. Oh yeah, lots of good beer helps too!

Well good friends lead me to our good buddy Huckleberry. Huck's real name is Kenneth McBroom but everybody just calls him Huck. He is from the great state of Tennessee; I call it a great state because they just happen to make some pretty good whiskey down there!

He loves to fish and usually shows up in town about the same time as the first Kings and leaves when all of the runs are well over. But this year he decided to try to make a run of living here full time.

We were all starting to get pretty buggy after several months without fishing so we decided to get together and rip it up.

After a great dinner filled with fishing and hunting lies and way too much scotch we decided to play a little poker. Just for fun of course!

Well after a couple of hours and a damn good thrashing at the table Huck decided it was time to change his luck so he jumped up from the table and ran backwards in circles around the table! Insisting that this was definitely going to change his luck.

It didn't so he tried it again in the other direction with the same effect. We were laughing so hard we all had tears in our eyes!

Every three or four hands up he would jump and the tears would start all over again.

By the end of the night he was completely broke so I bought his rain jacket from him so he had enough money to go out to the bar. I don't know if his luck got any better at the bar but with the streak he was on I doubt it.

We invited him back for poker several times after that but he never seemed to be available. Gee, I wonder why.

Murphy's law, I think...

A buddy of mine called me up a few weeks ago and let me know that I would be taking his nephew fishing while he was out of town on vacation. Since he had taken my nephew out the previous year I decided this was fair and agreed. Besides fishin' is fishin' no matter who are with you! Tori Frye arrived and it was time to fish.

The first day he was in town we targeted King Salmon. We trolled for five and a half hours without even a bump. We threw everything we could think of at those damn fish! Fish on top, fish down deep, flasher, no flasher, hook the herring backwards, everything! We chewed the fat and watched every other boat on the water catch at least one King. I was beginning to think that this boy had brought some bad fish mojo up from Seattle and we were going to have to take him out behind the shed and sacrifice him to the fish gods! We simply could not have any bad mojo!!!

Well we called it a day and made plans for early the next morning. Our luck was bound to change then, Cindy and the dogs were going with us and she is a fish magnet!

The next day I decided that we would go after halibut instead of salmon. The water was just beginning to have a little chop to it but the direction it was coming from made me believe that if we were willing to take a pretty good beating on the way when we turned the corner at Icy Straits we would be rewarded with smooth sailing. When I say a "pretty good beating" I am referring to the equivalent of a good old-fashioned Singapore cane thrashing!

On the way we told Tori how great this hole was and how to fish it. Just send your bait down to the bottom and bounce it three times and boom you will have a fish! He looked at us like we were crazy! I know he was thinking that we simply must be drinking way too much! His "Load of Crap" meter was really going off at that point!!!

Well we took our licks for forty-five minutes and there it was…the frog pond of our dreams! It was so flat and beautiful and one of the local charter boats was already on the site we were looking for so it was like it was meant to be!

We pulled up to the hole and I started dropping the anchor and I told Cindy and Tori to get the gear down and catch a fish.

Tori started messing with his gear and Cindy grabbed a halibut rod and started sending it down when she said, "Hey there is something wrong with this reel!" I took the rod from her and the year old reel just fell apart in my hands! Oh I was so pissed! And speaking of pissed; I really needed to go to the bathroom but that was not the time! It would just have to wait.

I told her to try the other halibut rod and that reel too had issues! I managed to get it to work and she started her way down to the bottom. Tori was still fumbling with his gear. I looked up and saw the flotilla of charter boats blasting towards us from Hoonah and realized that I would have to continue waiting to relieve myself. Oh well it's time to fish anyway.

Cindy hit bottom and I reminded her to bounce the bait three times and she did and wham! She had a halibut! She started bringing it up and Tori had a look of complete disbelief on his face!

She landed a nice 35-pound halibut and she handed me the rod to take a turn. Tori finally hit the bottom and got a bite but lost the fish and started bringing his line back in to re-bait.

I hit bottom and a halibut gladly jumped on my line, right on cue and I started bringing it up. This fish had some fight and I could tell that it had some real size to it but about half the way up I became distracted by my every growing need to empty my bladder and lost the damn fish!

Now there were way too many charter boats around to go. I just didn't think it was appropriate to show all of the tourists around us my "Fly Rod"! So I had to wait some more. Back down to the bottom with the bait.

Tori had finally hooked a fish. He was working it up. He and Cindy let it go since it was just a ping-pong paddle and he went back down again.

I hooked another fish and landed about a 25-pounder and went back down again. I asked Cindy if she wanted to take a turn but she was still tired from the first fish.

I got snagged on the bottom and had to cut the line. This was not good. I was not sure if we still had enough line on the reel to get back down again. I rigged it up and took the chance and just as it hit bottom there were three little raps of line left on the reel. Well we could keep fishing but we better not have one run on us! Also I noticed that about two feet past the end of the rod the line has started to unravel! If we happened to catch anything we would really have to nurse it the first few feet!

Well about that time Tori became snagged and had to cut his line. He definitely did not have enough line to continue so he had to start fishing with a salmon rod! Now it's gonna get fun!

I went down a couple of more times and managed to get snagged again. If it didn't pull free this time we were done for the day. Some how it did pull free and when the jig came out of the water there was a line hanging from the hook so I grabbed that line and started pulling it up. Some how on the end of that line was the jig that I had lost just an hour prior! What are the odds of that? Too bad we don't have a lottery I would have definitely bought a ticket that day!

Well I caught another small halibut and nursed it up to the top. At this point I really did not care who was around, I had to cast my "Fly Rod"! So I did and it was all good! Did I happen to mention that my "Fly Rod" is a 10 weight? Oh never mind! I did happen to get a really fine look from one of the charter boat captains but it had to be!

Tori managed to ease up two more halibut from the depths with his salmon rod and we were limited out!

We had a fine lunch and pulled the anchor and did a little salmon fishing while we were there. Tori caught a nice Chum and it was time to pay our penance to the fishing gods for all of the fish we had dispatched.

The ensuing hour and fifteen minute ride back, yes the water was much worse this time around, involved a much more intense version of the good old-fashioned Singapore cane thrashing we had experienced earlier!

Oh yeah! Another great day in the Great Land!

Six butt's in one day! Oh yeah!

Road trip time again…

Well we decided it was time for another friendly diversion into Canada so we loaded up the bike, that's right I said motorcycle, and blasted out of town. The plan was to take the new fast ferry up to Skagway and then ride all the way up to Dawson City. Take in the sights and maybe, just maybe, do a little fishing along the way. If the forest fires would allow, at this time there were over 150 wild fires burning throughout Alaska and the Yukon Territory.

The new fast ferry is awesome! It shaves the trip from Juneau to Skagway down to a mere two and a half hours! I highly recommend this method of getting to or leaving Juneau. The boat is nice, comfortable, and fast!

Once we arrived in Skagway we hopped on and headed for Whitehorse in the Yukon Territory. The road mirrors the old White Pass Rail Road that carried fortune seekers to the gold rush back in 1898. About halfway up the pass to the Canadian border the ceiling dropped on us and the ride was challenging at best. The temperature was about 35 degrees and the cloud that engulfed us bounced off of our helmets like we were driving through the film you find in ice trays that have only been in the freezer for about an hour and a half.

I knew things would get a lot better once we started down the other side of the pass and I was right. On the back side of the pass the temps shot right on up into the eighties and we were shuckin' gear left and right!

Time to lose some clothes!

We overnighted in Whitehorse and found out that the forest fires were going to change our plans just a bit. The wind was out of the south so Whitehorse was clear and warm but Dawson City was another story. Since I had no desire to smell like a smoked salmon we decided to stay in Whitehorse and fish the mighty Yukon River.

We tried our luck from shore for a few hours without even a bump. Must have been the gear we decided…couldn't possibly be us! So we ran back into town to consult with the local experts. Well we were using all of the same gear they suggested so I guess it really was just us!

Cindy fishin' the mighty Yukon!

We spent the rest of the day just taking in the sights of Whitehorse. One of the best sights we took in was when we had the pleasure of meeting one of the town's biggest celebrities, Boomer the dog.

RIP SOME LIPS

Meet Boomer!

Boomer is a mixed breed that was rescued from the local humane society several years ago. He looks pretty much like a giant Scottie dog on steroids! When Boomer was about a year old he lost a foot in a trap, a lot of fur trapping is still done in that area. So he does not get around very well but his person makes sure he is well taken care of and he is quite a character! His picture is on the Whitehorse Humane Society's website. If you ever get to Whitehorse you just might run into him at the park by the sternwheeler S.S. Klondike.

It's the S.S. Klondike.

The next day we decided to take a canoe trip down the river and try that angle. This turned out to be a great idea. I did the brunt of the rowing and Cindy fished all the way down the river. She didn't catch anything but then again neither did I!

As we were drifting down that massive river I could not help but imagine what it must have been like for the gold seekers making that same voyage 106 years ago. The Yukon is so beautiful and captivating it is simply amazing!

Trolling on the Yukon.

We only saw two other canoes on this trip and it was soooo cheap. $70 bucks to relive a piece of history, how could you go wrong? The van picked us up, right on time, and took us back to town for another fantastic dinner.

There's as old saying in Alaska that says you are not really an Alaskan until you have killed a bear and pissed in the Yukon River. Or is it made love in the Yukon River... well, either way I'm now a real Alaskan!

The next morning the winds had shifted and we were now in the smoker. It was time to run so we loaded up the bike and headed for Atlin.

On the road to Atlin we had a robin try to kill us! We were cruising along at 65 mph when that damn bird became indecisive. I saw it coming. It swooped right in front of us and turned and seemed to just hover right about chest level! I just gritted my teeth and thought, "Oh shit...that's gonna hurt!" But at the last second, not an exaggeration, it darted off to the right and I was spared a killer mark!

Once we checked into our "B & B", I'll discuss that a little later, we headed for the fishing grounds. As I have mentioned before Atlin is one of the world's premier fly fishing destinations. With Grayling, Rainbow, Pike, and Lake Trout how could you miss?

We headed out to the stream that flows from Surprise Lake and got into the Grayling. Cindy was yanking them in left and right. I was only able to land one but with constant action who cares?

Cindy loves her Grayling!

We gave the fish a rest and beat feet for town. We couldn't afford to miss dinner since there is only one restaurant in town. Miss dinner and you are just out of luck!

Then it was back to our room for a well needed night of rest. Now correct me if I am wrong but aren't the two prerequisites of being a "B & B" having a bed and serving breakfast? Well after our long day on the road, almost being killed by a robin, and a strenuous evening of fishing we finally plopped down on our bed. Holy crap! Our bed was the equivalent of a washcloth being draped over a pile of railroad ties! The leaders of the Spanish Inquisition would have been proud of this device. We started calling it the "Rack & Breakfast"! There was absolutely no way of lying on this "bed" in a comfortable position. And we could not dull the pain and try to pass out by drinking alcohol because the liquor store in Atlin closed at 5pm! What kind of a liquor store closes at 5pm? Hell, that's when I'm just startin' to get rolling!

I decided to try to read myself to sleep. I reached over and turned on the "reading" lamp, not knowing that this too was folly. When I turned that switch it was like turning on the noonday sun! Who puts a 150 watt bulb in a reading lamp? So I saw the error in my ways and turned that switch again, hoping to turn the sun off only to find that this was a multi way lamp! Our room now looked like the flash one would see at a nuclear test site! "Please make it stop...please make it go away!" I thought! Here goes, one more attempt to turn it off...switch...SUPER NOVA!!! The words "GE 150 WATT" are now burned into my retinas so every time I close my eyes I have a little reminder of that wonderful "B & B"!

The only way it could possibly be any worse is if we had to stay another night. Oh yeah...we did! There were no other rooms available anywhere in town so the first thing we did the next morning was head to the liquor store for some medication to get us through the next night. After that it was off for more fishing.

We went over to Como Lake and got into the Rainbow Trout. We could see some really nice, 3-5 pounders but the only ones we could entice to bite were the little growlers. You know the kind, hold one in your hand and the head and tail is about all that sticks out. Oh well they were fun to catch anyway.

Around noon we went back into town for lunch and to check on some more gear. You can never have enough good gear.

That's when we met Pat. He was working at the local fishing shop and was full of great information. After talking to him for about an hour he said, "Hell, why don't you just go fishing with me? We will take the boat out on Lake Atlin and go for Lake Trout." We jumped at the chance.

While we were waiting to head out Pat got a call that a friend had been in some sort of an accident so he had to run and check in on him. This delayed our outing by a few hours and when Pat got back he told us all about his friends "accident".

It seems that his friend and his dog were making their way back to the cabin they were staying at when their camp was attacked by a pack of wolves. The wolves came in the tent and he and the dog went out the side of it. On the way out he pepper sprayed some of the wolves and himself pretty well and ran for a tree. He watched the wolves kill his dog and was stuck in the tree for two days waiting for the wolves to lose interest! Apparently, he will be all right, in time, but he had to be transported to Whitehorse for treatment. Only in the North!

Anyway Pat made it back with his trusty first mate "Sarah the dog" and it was time to fish. He must have called her "Sarah the dog" at least five hundred times that night!

It's Sarah the Dog!

Atlin Lake is an absolutely beautiful lake. It's huge and clear as looking into a glass of spring water. It's all glacier fed, from the Juneau ice fields, and you can literally see fifty or sixty feet down! Just gorgeous!

Pat told us to run our lines down to the bottom, so we did and we started to troll. After about an hour he said we should bring our lines in and "clear the weeds. Speaking of weed…I've been known to smoke a little weed…would you mind if I did just that?" I said, "Dude it's your boat." He smiled and we made for shore. He and "Sarah the dog" took a little "nature walk" and came on back to the boat.

When we launched again I decided that this was just going to be a sightseeing trip, with our captain in this condition we probably were not going to have much luck anyway so we kicked back and enjoyed the view. We saw a beautiful mule deer that seemed to really be interested in what we were doing. That deer watched us for a good twenty minutes. We also had three loons swim right up to the boat.

All in all it was a great evening and next time we head for Atlin we will take our skiff so we can fish that lake right.

Well it was back to the "Rack and Breakfast" for another night of torture! Even that bed could not ruin our day. Atlin is a must for anyone that loves the outdoors.

The next morning we were back on the bike for Skagway. The ride was fantastic. We finally got to see the top of White Pass. No clouds this time and it is truly an awesome sight. It is a very strange place; all of the trees are in miniature, due to the harsh weather up there. It looks like you have been plucked up by a UFO and placed in the middle of some alien model train set! Very cool.

Then after a night in Skagway, drinking at the Red Onion it was time to get on the ferry for our trip back to Juneau. What a great little diversion!

That had to hurt...

We had heard that the silvers were in early so it was time to target those slimy buggers! Cindy, Remington, Whiskey, and I loaded up the boat and headed out for Hand Trollers Cove on the back side of Shelter Island.

When we arrived the water was a little choppy but not too bad so down went the lines. Within fifteen minutes one of the rods took off and I was reeling in a really puny little silver. I shook him off and sent the line back down.

We kept getting bites but no fish. Those slick bastards were gorging themselves on our bait and spittin' out the hooks! After re-baiting at least eight or ten times we finally found some that were a little more suicidal!

The rod jumped into life and I set the hook just as that fish broke the surface. The fight was on! He jumped and danced on the water just like Savion Glover would if he could!

Cindy netted him and the skunk was off the boat.

We took turns doing this silver dance three more times with the same result. Oh it's gonna be a good year…lot's of smoked salmon all winter long!

I love catching silvers because they are so active. Short runs and lot's of splashin' about. What more could you want? Kings are fun too with that bull run to the bottom but silvers make me happy.

Speaking of that "bull run", the next rod to take off did just that! Cindy said, "Gimme that rod! It's a King and I want it!" Well I jumped out of the way so I wouldn't end up in the drink and let her have it.

That fish ran hard and long, just like a King. Every time she would start to make a little headway he would go for another run. Great fish!

Finally he started to tire and Cindy was able to get him up to the boat. But wait, that didn't look right? He was coming up to the boat backwards!

Cindy shouted, "I hooked him in the bunghole! I hooked him in the bunghole!" And he ran again. I guess I too would run like a King or Carl Lewis or Michael Johnson if I was hooked in the bunghole! Yikes! That had to hurt!

Well we finally got him in the boat and he was bleeding pretty good so we couldn't let him go. He was terminal, so his fate was sealed. His destiny was the smoker. But I would probably be terminal too if I was just hooked in the bunghole and dragged through the water for fifteen minutes!

After one more fish, caught in the mouth I might add. It was time to call it a day. What a great time and I now have a whole new respect for hemorrhoid sufferers!

Backward ass silvers...oh boy!!!

Yes they do...

I'm sure you have heard the old quip in response to a stupid question, "Do bears shit in the woods?" Well I'm here to tell you that the answer is yes they do! Huge steaming piles filled with blue berries, sticks, and anything else they have been eating. When you are in bear country on a hunt believe me you take note.

Not long ago Cindy and I were over in Hoonah on a deer hunt and we noticed that there was an abnormal amount of scat. It was everywhere and it was huge! Scary huge! So we were really being careful, to say the least.

The hunt was proceeding in the normal fashion. Lot's of deer...pick and choose the ones you wanted. You gotta love Hoonah it usually is that way. The bears obviously are not putting a dent in that population.

Anyway we were on a three day hunt and it was mid-September so the leaves had not dropped off the trees yet. Not the best thing when you are hiking on Chicagoff Island.

The first morning we popped a nice deer for the freezer. We woke up, left camp, and there it was. Neat and sweet. I got the thing dressed and we packed it back to the truck for safe keeping. We were gone no more than fifteen minutes and when we went back past that site the gut pile was gone! Holy crap! That damn Ursa must have been watching me dress it out! Not the most comforting feeling.

I decided right there and then that I was not going to act like a bear and shit in the woods! No how…no way! Not gonna let Yogi catch me with my pants down! I could make it three days. No problem! Cindy agreed so it was settled, no one was going to take a dump for the next three days!

Well we passed on several nice deer looking for that perfect one, of course and soon it was nightfall. We made camp and had a terrific dinner and called it a night.

Day two came around and we bagged a nice buck only to have the same thing happen. I think we were being stalked by that brownie!

Day two also brought the beginnings of the self-imposed bear constipation. Gonna have to quit eating, I guess.

The hunt continued, without any luck, as did the search for relief.

Day three and there was no denying the inevitable! I had to go! For the first time in my entire life I wanted to drop trow in the middle of the biggest field I could find. To Hell with modesty, I wanted to be able to see that sucker coming and I really didn't care who saw me download that file!

Cindy and I took turns standing guard while the other did the deed. But I have to tell you it takes real talent to wipe your ass while squatting in the middle of a field while holding a .338 and trying not to get you know what all over the pants you have around your ankles!

We didn't see anymore deer on that trip but we both did learn that our multi-tasking skills are beyond compare!!!

The four that got away...

My wife called me up and told me that I was going to take a couple of guys fishing last weekend. I agreed not realizing that they were touchy feely Greenpeace-esque California types. Well that's not fair, only one of them was a touchy feely Greenpeace-esque California type!

Don was great but Kevin "The Liberator" was a whole other story! Why is he "The Liberator"? Well almost every time we hooked up he would "liberate" that fish somehow! Let the line go slack...set the hook like he was trying to pull start a D-8! You get the picture.

The first day we managed to land eight nice Silvers. We actually caught about twenty but you can refer to the last paragraph to see what happened to the other twelve.

"The Liberator" wanted to be "hands on" in the entire process. He wanted to learn about everything. So I agreed and taught him how to cut the bait. Hook the bait. Run the lines. He loved it. He just soaked it up. Little did I know that his "hands on" assistance would prove to be our downfall!

Oh I almost forgot, on the first day we also had Scott on the boat. Scott was really hung over and was an absolute Pink Salmon magnet. Every time he grabbed a rod it was a Pink. Nice enough guy, I guess, all he really did was nurse crackers into his mouth and catch pinks.

Hung over boy catches a Silver!

The next day it was just Don, Cindy, myself, and "The Liberator" and the day started out exactly the same. Hook up and let Kevin lose the fish! He lost the first four fish of the day. Don finally took a turn and big surprise we actually caught a fish. It was a really small Silver so I took my turn at being "The Liberator" and set it free. This obviously pleased the fish gods because not ten minutes later one of the rods took off and there was no doubt about what was on that line. It was screamin' with the sound of a King Salmon!

Against my better judgment I gave the rod to "The Liberator" and he managed to actually catch the fish! A beautiful 28 1/2 inch King! Not a lot of weight but a beauty for sure.

I guess that being a fish liberator is like a disease, you catch it on your finger tips and it crawls right up your sleeves! Thanks Lyle Lovett! Don had a bout with this terrible malady. He hooked into a really nice King and fought that beast for about five minutes before it was able to free it's self. We did get to see it and it was a great fish. We all agreed that it was Kevin's fault that we lost that fish as well.

We managed to land four more Silvers before "The Liberator" struck again!

Don lands the fateful sixth fish of the day!

Don had just landed the sixth fish of the day and I was baiting the line back up when that touchy feely Greenpeace-esque California type reared his ugly head again. He said he was going to put the fish on the stringer while I was busy with the rod and I looked over at him and said "Fine but don't lose those frickin' fish!" and I turned back to my task. Then there was this overwhelming feeling of doom and a moment of complete silence. The kind of silence that only occurs when evil is afoot! Like when you all of a sudden realize that you can't hear the kids or the dogs and you just know that someone or something is poopin' on your new rug! I couldn't even hear the kicker! I turned to see what was causing that great feeling of doom and saw Kevin "The Liberator" standing at the back of the boat holding the two ends of the stringer with a look of total disbelief on his halibut pale face. Then I saw four of our fish wafting back down to the bottom of the sea! Holy crap! He had liberated our dead fish! He had done the one thing I had told him not to do! I just started to laugh like Jack Nicholson in The Shinning! What else could I do!

The Liberator…way to go!

The good news is I now have a new lot in life. As long as I live I will do my best to never let him forget that he is "The Liberator"! Maybe Arnold Schwarzenegger was right…California is full of "Girlie Men"!

Don is welcome back anytime but Kevin "The Liberator" better bring really good scotch, and a lot of it, if he wants to come back!

The Fish-o-matic...

Cindy's father had wanted to come up and fish the Golden North Salmon Derby with us for quite some time so I agreed. But only if he brought a playmate, someone to entertain him some of the time so I could get a bit of relief. When the rules were laid out he jumped at the chance to spend some quality time with one of his cousins Pat Barnes. So the Alvin Keely and Pat Barnes road show blew into town!

We took them out for a trial run on the Thursday evening before the Derby and I found out just what was in store. They were going to "help" me every chance they could.

Every time I picked up a hook to bait it up someone just so happened to grab that rod and give it a good yank to try to help. Well, if you are wondering what happens when a rod is yanked while you are putting bait on the hook, I'm here to tell you it ain't pretty! There is nothing like pulling 3/0 hooks out of your fingers, palms, wrists, legs, well I think you get the picture! I was bleedin' like a Pink when it hits the deck!

Being the good "charter boat" captain that I am I could not say anything. Not to mention the fact that he is my father-in-law! Just grin and bear it! That's all I could do! I cursed those "helpful" old dudes for days! Anyway that night we managed to pick up a couple of nice Silvers and a few Pinks and had quite a few laughs.

The next two days of the Derby flew by. We caught Silvers and Pinks left and right or I should say we lost Silvers and Pinks left and right but we landed enough to still have a good time. Alvin told stories about Pat and Pat told Alvin he was lying and fun was had by all!

By day three of the Derby, let's just say, I was growing tired of all of the "help". I do believe it is fair to say that I was starting to get a little grumpy! My hands looked like they had been run through some gadget that Ronco would be selling at three in the morning on some cable channel! But the good news was they were finally beginning to catch and land more fish than they were losing! Yeah!

Alvin hooked into a fish and fought it up to the side of the boat so I leaned over to see if it was a Silver or a Pink to decide if I needed the net or the gaff. If it was a Silver I would grab the net so we could keep it and if it was a Pink I would just use the gaff and let the beast go. Well, I saw that it was a Pink and told Pat to give me the gaff and then watched Alvin lead that poor fish right into the prop of the kicker. It was spectacular! That fish shot through that prop just like a cuisinart food processor! Buzz! The Alvin Fish-o-matic was invented! The back of the boat boiled with blood and former Pink parts! I told Pat that I was not going to need that gaff after all.

We continued to fish and caught our limit on Silvers but nothing big enough to place in the Derby.

Alvin, Pat, Kevin and a mess of Silvers!!!

The next day the guys flew out to Admiralty Island for a few days of trout fishing. They stayed in one of the forestry cabins out there and caught a fair share of trout. This is a diversion I strongly recommend. The cabins are really cheap and the wilderness experience is unmatched. The old saying is that you don't really get to see Alaska until you get to the end of the road. Another reason I really recommend this is it gets your guests out of your hair for a few days! Ha ha!

They fished and smoked and drank and played dominoes for days. Pat said that he never wanted to see another set of dominoes again. They had a great time.

It was truly a great weekend but maybe that is just the loss of blood talking. No it really was a great time and I look forward to another visit from those two crazy old dudes!

I don't want any part of that...

Last week we made our annual pilgrimage over to Hoonah for a grocery run. Grocery run, you ask? Well that is what we call our deer hunting trips. It's time to subsist, gather, harvest, and be manly men or manly women. Trust me after four days in the woods even the most girlie girl can get pretty manly! Woo baby...I can smell ya!

Well the hunt went just as planned. The four of us were able to pop a total of six nice deer. Yes we discovered Deer Valhalla where only huge deer are allowed to play! And we found some great new places to go fly fishing next year. We also saw an incredible amount of brown bears. And the weather was awesome...what more could you possibly want?

Margie and Frank exit Deer Valhalla!!!

As I have mentioned before we like to name the fish, crab, or furry little critters that we dispatch. I know it is sick but it is our own version of Alaskan Therapy. So watch out! If you piss me off you can bet I will club, boil, or shoot something that is named after you!

Our good friends, Margie and Frank Byrd plugged a deer that will always be remembered as "Buddy". No one named "Buddy" pissed us off it's just that when "Buddy" was sent to the other side another deer was standing right next to him. We imagine "Buddy's" friend was saying something like this, "Come on Buddy…let's get out of here! There's something wrong. Come on Buddy…please get up! Buddy!!!"

Later on in the trip I came across another pair of deer standing together and yes I have to admit it…I shot the Olsen Twins! Later I ate the Olsen Twins but that is whole other story! Yes the Olsen Twins do piss me off. No one should be that young and that rich! Besides I think they both could use a sandwich and a KitKat bar!

Anyway after skinning the Olsen Twins and returning back to Juneau it was time to get those deer in the freezer. Well we hung them up in the garage and decided to let the dogs come on down so the whole family could be together. Besides we have a saying…the family that slays together stays together!

Whiskey, the Scottie, just wanted to devour the two deer. No question about it she let us know that she was up to the task.

Remington, our lab, was a whole other issue. He came in very cautiously. Ears back and tail down. Labs have a way of telling you exactly what they are thinking at any given moment and his face was telling a tale. In his eyes I could tell that he was thinking, "Pa, this is just waaaay too close to home for me! Those things look just like me! I don't want any part of that! They must have really been bad for Pa to do that! Please make this bad dream go away!"

Just for fun I pointed my knife at Rem and said, "Boy, this is what happens to bad dogs!" Cindy then told me, "Don't say that...you know he understands everything you say!"

After the Olsen Twins were cut up his happy go lucky demeanor came back and everything was okay. Yet another great weekend in the Great Land!

About the Author

J. Kevin Curry loves to hunt and fish in the Great Land. He enjoys sharing his adventures with friends, family, or anyone else silly/brave enough to share his passions. As he likes to say, "There are only two kinds of people in Alaska, those that absolutely love it and those that absolutely hate it! And those that hate it usually don't stick around too long and we don't want them here anyway!" If you have not guessed he absolutely loves it!

They say that you are not an Alaskan until you have killed a bear and pissed in the Yukon River. Well he has and therefore he is!

J. Kevin Curry makes his home in beautiful Juneau, Alaska. There he hunts, fishes, brews beer, and drinks beer with his wife Cindy and their two dogs Remington and Whiskey.

Printed in the United States
57615LVS00001B/247-357